THE HOMESTEAD ACT

A **TRUE BOOK**®

by

Elaine Landau

Children's Press®

A Division of Scholastic Inc.

New York Toronto London Auckland Sydney

Inside a sod house
at Nebraska's Sod
House Museum

Content Consultant
Edward Soza
Author and Historian

Reading Consultant
Dr. Cecilia Minden-Cupp
*Former Director, Language
and Literacy Program
Harvard Graduate School
of Education*

Author's Dedication
For Klara Sweeney

*The illustration on the cover
shows settlers crossing the
Great Plains. The photograph
on the title page shows a sod
house in Nebraska.*

Library of Congress Cataloging-in-Publication Data
Landau, Elaine.
   The Homestead Act / by Elaine Landau.
      p. cm. — (A True Book)
   Includes bibliographical references and index.
   ISBN 0-516-25870-2 (lib. bdg.)   0-516-27902-5 (pbk.)
      1. Frontier and pioneer life—West (U.S.)—Juvenile literature. 2.
Homestead law—West (U.S.)—History—19th century—Juvenile literature.
3. Land settlement—West (U.S.)—History—19th century—Juvenile litera-
ture. 4. Public lands—West (U.S.)—History—19th century—Juvenile litera-
ture. 5. West (U.S.)—History—1860–1890—Juvenile literature. I. Title.
II. Series.
F596.L359 2006
978'.02—dc22   2005020407

Contents

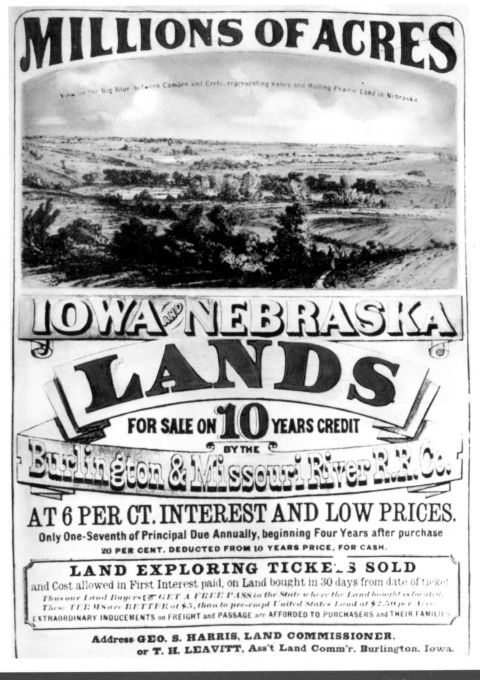

Posters encouraged farmers to move west. This poster from a railroad company advertises cheap land.

Building America

LAND BONANZA!
MILLIONS OF ACRES
FREE TO HOMESTEADERS

During the mid-1860s, posters and newspaper ads like this one were seen everywhere. The United States was still growing. The first Europeans to come to America had built

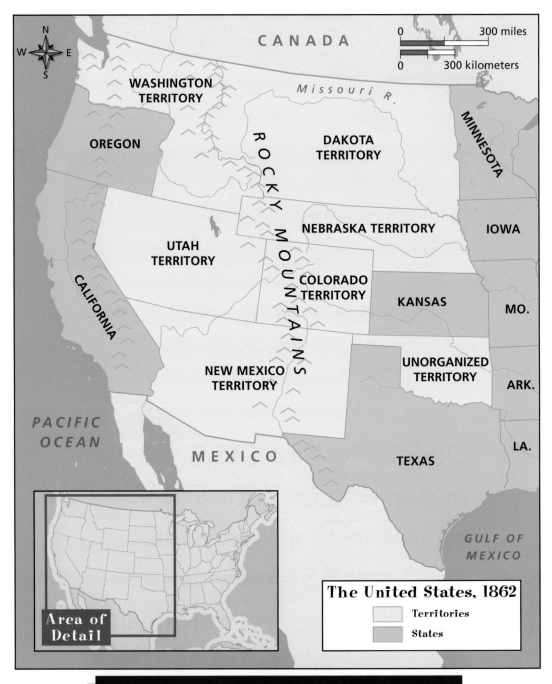

A map of the United States the year the Homestead Act was passed

up the East. In time, large numbers of people headed west to California and Oregon. They went in search of gold or rich farmland.

A vast part of the country remained unsettled, however. The grassy area between Missouri and the Rocky Mountains was still wide open. This was Indian territory.

Treaties with the U.S. government had given American Indians the right to remain on

Elk feed on the grasslands of the United States.

this land. Yet by the 1860s, the government no longer wanted an unsettled region separating the country's East and West. Most whites did not respect the Indians. They wanted this region settled by people like themselves. So U.S. government leaders broke the treaties. They forced the Indians to move to areas of land known as **reservations**.

Many American Indians were forced to move to reservations.

Families packed their things and headed west with hopes for a better life.

The removal of Indians opened the region for more white settlements. Now the government needed to draw people to this new **frontier**. That would not be easy.

Settling any wilderness could be difficult and dangerous. Countless hours of backbreaking work and a great deal of sacrifice would be necessary.

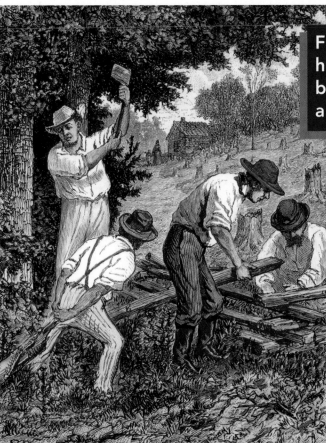

Frontier life required hard work, such as building fences around a homestead.

The settlers would have to leave behind many relatives and friends. They would also have to leave behind established towns and occupy large stretches of emptiness.

Many people avoided this region for another reason. They mistakenly thought of it as a dry wasteland. For years, it had been improperly called the Great American Desert. But early settlers soon found that crops such as corn and wheat grew well in parts of the area.

Early settlers were pleased to find the open land often had rich soil.

Some members of the U.S. Congress argued that those taming this wilderness were patriots. They were helping

The Homestead Act gave free land to citizens such as these future homesteaders, registering at canvas tents in Oklahoma Territory in 1893.

their country grow. The government wanted to make it easier for others to do the same. It decided to give away land to those willing to develop it. These individuals would pay only a small fee to claim the property. In return, they would receive a **homestead.**

It was an exciting plan that could benefit many Americans. It would be achieved through a new law known as the Homestead Act of 1862.

A Chance for Change

Many people saw the Homestead Act of 1862 as a wonderful opportunity. A man or woman of any race who was at least twenty-one years old and the head of a house-hold could receive 160 acres (65 hectares) of free land. That person had to be a U.S.

The Homestead Act helped these four sisters own land on the frontier.

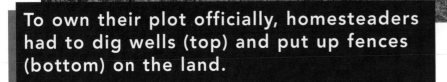

To own their plot officially, homesteaders had to dig wells (top) and put up fences (bottom) on the land.

citizen who had never fought against the country. Newcomers to America who intended to become citizens could apply for homesteads as well.

To own the property permanently, homesteaders had to live on the land for at least five years and **prove up**, or develop it. Developing the land meant building a home, digging a well, farming a number of acres, and fencing in part of the homestead.

President Abraham Lincoln
signed the Homestead Act on
May 20, 1862. It opened a door
for poor people in the East and
Midwest who might never have
been able to be landowners.
Now they could own a farm.

African Americans and women could become landowners as well. A number of former slaves applied for homesteads. Owning their own farms became an important symbol of independence for them.

An African-American family poses for a photograph on their homestead in Nebraska.

Under the Homestead Act of 1862, **widows** were considered heads of households, too. They applied for homesteads and started some very successful farms.

The Homestead Act of 1862 drew large numbers of **immigrants**, or newcomers, to the frontier. Often these people had come to the United States from Europe seeking a better life for themselves and their families. Numerous

On the stamp: **NORGE** · UTVANDRINGEN TIL AMERIKA · 125 · S. MORKEN 1975

A Norwegian postage stamp, based on this photograph of a homesteading family from Norway, honors the 150th anniversary of Norwegians coming to the United States to start new lives.

Norwegians, Germans, and Swedes became homesteaders. Other immigrant groups followed.

In time, homesteaders traveled west on the railroads.

Through the years, eager homesteaders continued to arrive. Newly completed railroad lines helped bring these settlers and their supplies to the area. The Homestead Act of 1862 eventually changed the face of the American frontier.

First to File

A Union army scout named Daniel Freeman is thought to have been the first person to file a land claim under the Homestead Act of 1862. Freeman settled in Beatrice, Nebraska. The site of his claim is now the Homestead National Monument of America.

Daniel Freeman

A New Life

The new homesteaders faced a big challenge. They had come to an area that looked like an endless sea of grass. There were hardly any trees on the **prairie.** After the first homesteaders claimed the few wooded spots near rivers and creeks, most homesteaders

This photograph of a sod house was taken in Nebraska in 1901.

had little wood for building a home.

Yet they soon found a way around this problem. They built sod houses known as **soddies.**

These homes were made of dirt and grass bricks cut from the soil. Such houses were plain and rough. Usually a whole family lived in one small room. There was little privacy or space to be alone.

Often after a heavy rain, the roofs made of straw or branches leaked, turning the dirt floors to mud. Soddies also had their share of mice, bugs, and snakes. The home-steaders never knew what would come out of their dirt walls. As soon as most home-steaders could put aside enough money, they bought lumber. As time passed, they replaced their sod homes with wood-frame houses.

The lack of wood on the prairie also meant a lack of fuel. Yet the settlers could not survive without fire for both warmth and cooking. So they learned to burn buffalo chips. Buffalo chips were dried pieces of buffalo droppings. Women and children sometimes spent hours collecting these chips from the ground.

A mother collects buffalo chips with her daughter on the plains.

Having enough water for their families was very important to homesteaders. Soon after arriving, they would dig a well. But water, like lumber, was difficult to come by, and not all wells

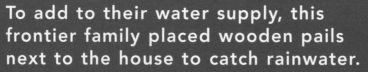
To add to their water supply, this frontier family placed wooden pails next to the house to catch rainwater.

reached water. Pioneer life was especially tough for these families. They had to collect rainwater in barrels and buckets. Unfortunately, flies, mosquitoes, and dust usually collected in these containers as well.

Because water was scarce, most settlers bathed only once a week. The whole family had to share the same dirty bath-water. Afterward, the settlers used it for household cleaning.

Homesteaders worked hard to have enough food. Most families planted vegetable gardens with seeds they had brought with them. They counted on these small gardens for part of their food supply. Homesteaders gathered and ate wild plants and berries, too.

Because these homesteaders had gone west to farm, they also planted crops. Fields of corn and wheat soon dotted the area. The homesteaders sold these crops for cash. They also kept some of the crops for their families to eat.

Everyone worked hard on a homestead. These pioneers made nearly everything themselves, and

Even young pioneer children helped feed animals, milk cows, and do other chores.

there was much to do. People got up early in the morning and worked until dark.

Children were expected to do their part. They helped their parents with the chores. Boys

Everyone pitched in around the farm.

usually plowed the fields with their fathers. Girls tended the vegetable gardens and helped with the cooking, washing, and housework. At times, the women worked alongside the men in the fields, too.

Schools Sprang Up

By the 1880s, homesteaders began building schools for their children, called one-room school-houses. All of the children in the school sat in the same room with only one teacher. A homesteader's children did not always attend school. They went to school only when they were not needed at home. That meant they were usually not in class during the planting and harvesting seasons.

A one-room sod schoolhouse in Kansas

The End of an Era

While everyone headed for the frontier with high hopes, not all homesteaders succeeded. Some who had come from cities had little farming experience and soon failed. At times, even good farmers did poorly. Insects, **droughts**, and prairie fires ruined crops.

Homesteaders told stories of how grasshoppers ate whole fields of corn.

Some farm families had trouble being so far away from other people. At first, there were no schools or churches to attend. Plus they lived too far from other homesteaders to visit often or develop close friendships.

In the end, only half of the homesteaders stayed long enough to earn the right to keep their property under the rules of the Homestead Act of 1862. Other families did

This modern farm in Idaho started out as a homestead.

extremely well and not only received deeds to their property, but were able to add more acres to their land. They remained in the area for years to come.

By 1900, homesteaders had claimed 80 million acres (32 million ha) of land. Farms, towns, and people now replaced wilderness. Out of this region came the states of Nebraska, Montana, North Dakota, South Dakota, Oklahoma, Wyoming, New Mexico, Colorado, and others.

The Homestead Act of 1862 served its purpose. The homesteaders' hard work paid off. These families helped build America.

Many of today's U.S. cities, including Denver, Colorado, owe some of their success to the country's first homesteaders.

To Find Out More

Here are some additional resources to help you learn more about the Homestead Act:

 **Books**

Bial, Raymond. **Frontier Home.** Houghton Mifflin, 1993.

Furbee, Mary Rodd. **Outrageous Women of the American Frontier.** John Wiley & Sons, 2002.

Gunderson, Mary. **Pioneer Farm Cooking: Exploring History Through Simple Recipes.** Blue Earth Books, 2000.

Kamma, Anne. **A Pioneer on the Prairie.** Scholastic, 2003.

Littlefield, Holly. **Children of the Trail West.** Carolrhoda, 1999.

Patent, Dorothy Hinshaw. **Homesteading: Settling America's Heartland.** Walker Books, 1998.

Organizations and Online Sites

Homestead National Monument of America

8523 West State Highway 4
Beatrice, NE 68310
402-223-3514
http://www.nps.gov/home/

Visit the national park that honors the historic Homestead Act. Go to the organization's site to read biographies of famous people with homesteading connections, including inventor George Washington Carver and author Laura Ingalls Wilder.

The Library of Congress, Today in History: May 20 (The Homestead Act)

http://memory.loc.gov/ ammem/today/may20.html

Check out this site for interesting information and photographs about the Homestead Act of 1862.

Pioneer Camera: Sod Houses

http://www.lib.ndsu.nodak. edu/ndirs/exhibitions/ pioneer/camera/sod.htm

Don't miss these fascinating pictures and descriptions of pioneer sod houses.

Seeds of Change Garden

http://www.mnh.si.edu/ archives/garden/history/ welcome.html

Many pioneers on the prairie grew corn and wheat. Learn more about these important crops here.

Important Words

droughts long periods of very dry weather

frontier the edge of an area that is still largely unsettled by people

homestead a piece of land given by the government to a settler

immigrants people who come to a new country to live there permanently

prairie a large grassy area with few trees

prove up to develop or improve land

reservations areas of land on which some American Indians were forced to live

soddies sod houses made of dirt and grass bricks cut from the soil

treaties formal agreements between groups, such as the U.S. government and Indian nations

widows women whose husbands have died